Pickleball
Pickleball
Pickleball

Pickleball Pickleball Pickleball

Skills, Rules, & Strategies
(A Pro's Guide)

by Riley J. Ford

Pickleball, Pickleball, Pickleball: Skills, Rules, & Strategies (A Pro's Guide) is the definitive resource for everyone, from beginners to seasoned players, looking to master the fast-growing sport of pickleball.

Are you a novice searching for clear explanations on the basic rules of pickleball? Or an advanced player striving to refine your strategy? This book offers a comprehensive breakdown, catering to every skill level. Through exclusive interviews with a seasoned pro, the author unlocks the secrets of the sport, offering insights and firsthand advice that will set you apart on the court.

Inside, you'll discover:
- **Foundational Skills:** Master the basics, including serving, returns, volleys, and the essential dink.
- **Rules & Etiquette:** A clear, concise overview ensuring you play with confidence and respect.

- **Advanced Strategies:** Step up your game with tactics and strategies used by pros.
- **Equipment Recommendations:** Navigate the myriad of paddles, balls, and court gear available.
- **Drills & Exercises:** Improve your agility, stamina, and precision with tried-and-tested drills.

Pickleball's popularity is soaring, making it essential to have the best resources at hand. Whether you're gearing up for competitive play, or just enjoying a casual game with friends, this book ensures you get the most out of every match.

Maximize your performance. Play with skill. Dive into the world of pickleball like never before.

Author's Note

Dear Reader,

In your hands is a book filled with insights directly from a top tier pickleball pro. While I had the privilege to interview and learn from this expert, they've chosen to remain anonymous. There are a few reasons for this: a strong preference for privacy, contractual obligations, the desire to keep the spotlight on the game rather than on an individual, and the ever-present challenges of modern-day public scrutiny.

While I honor their wish for anonymity, rest assured you're receiving gold-standard advice from the industry's best. Dive in and elevate your game!

Warmly,

Riley J. Ford
New York Times bestselling author

Contents

Introduction

Brief Overview

Importance of the sport in modern athletics and recreation

Pickleball's Ascendancy

- *Rapid Growth:* Pickleball's rapid growth is reflected in the numbers. With over 3.3 million participants in the U.S. by 2020, pickleball's rapid surge is evident in the mushrooming of specialized facilities and competitive events.
- *Inclusivity:* Tailored for everyone, from kids to seniors, and even those with disabilities, pickleball's allure lies in its accessibility and adaptability.
- *Physical and Mental Health:* Beyond its entertainment value, pickleball provides a cardiovascular workout, sharpens reflexes, and offers a dose of

mental wellness through its communal play and friendship.

- *Social Fabric:* In a world where loneliness is a growing concern, the team spirit of pickleball acts as a balm, forging connections and fostering community.
- *Economic Revival:* The sport's exponential growth paves the way for economic opportunities, from gear merchandising to tourism sparked by regional tournaments.
- *Modern Athletic Footprint:* Striking a balance between leisure and athleticism, pickleball has etched a significant mark in contemporary sports by harmoniously melding accessibility, camaraderie, and fitness.

In essence, pickleball is not just a game—it's a movement, shaping the very contours of modern athletics and community well-being.

Purpose and Audience
This guide delves deep into the world of pickleball, catering to a spectrum of enthu-

siasts—from novices seeking foundational knowledge to seasoned players craving advanced strategies.

Highlights of the book include professional insights, equipment recommendations, game tactics, and physical conditioning tips. Whether you're exploring a new hobby, aiming to sharpen your techniques, or a coach eyeing to integrate pickleball into your program, this book is your comprehensive companion, crafted to enrich your pickleball journey at every stage.

CHAPTER 1
The Origins of Pickleball

1.1 History of the Game

Did you know pickleball was born out of sheer boredom? That's right! One summer afternoon in 1965 on Bainbridge Island, Washington, three dads—Joel Pritchard, Barney McCallum, and Bill Bell—found themselves with restless kids and nothing to do. They improvised a game using available equipment: ping-pong paddles and a perforated ball. They lowered the net on a badminton court, and voila, pickleball was born! From a makeshift game to an international sensation, pickleball has come a long way.

1.2 How Pickleball Got Its Name

Ah, the pickle! Despite popular myths, pickleball is not named after the delicious, tangy snack. The name actually comes from "Pickles," a spaniel owned by co-founder

Joel Pritchard. Pickles had a knack for running off with the ball during games. So, when it came to naming the sport, "Pickle's ball" seemed fitting. Over time, it was shortened to the snappy "pickleball" we know today.

1.3 The Evolution of Rules and Equipment

In its early days, pickleball rules were somewhat of a work in progress. Players borrowed elements from badminton, tennis, and table tennis, creating a quirky hybrid. Over time, the rules got formalized, such as the unique "two-bounce rule" and the "non-volley zone," aka the "kitchen." Paddles have also evolved from simple wooden boards to high-tech composite materials designed for specific types of play. The balls have undergone a transformation too, from the original wiffle balls to ones specifically engineered for pickleball play.

1.4 The Rise in Popularity

Fast forward to today, and you'll find pickleball courts popping up like daisies—

from community centers to elite sports clubs. The sport's explosion isn't confined to the United States; it's catching fire globally! With over 3.3 million players in the U.S. alone as of 2020, pickleball tournaments and leagues are now as commonplace as weekend BBQs. People are "dinking" and "smashing" their way into a sport that has broken age barriers and captivated hearts. Some enthusiasts even jokingly call it a cult!

CHAPTER 2
Understanding the Basics

2.1 The Court

Dimensions

Ah, the pickleball court—a rectangle of possibilities! Measuring 20 feet by 44 feet, it's a tad smaller than a tennis court, which means less sprinting and more strategy. Trust me, it's the perfect size for an action-packed game without exhausting you two points in.

Lines and Zones

The court is a labyrinth of lines, but don't let that scare you! You've got your "baseline," where the serve is initiated, and the "non-volley line," a magical seven-foot zone extending from the net where—you guessed it—volleys are forbidden! This area is affectionately known as the "kitchen," but the only thing cooking there is your strategy to avoid stepping in this designated area (unless the ball bounces there first, of course...but more on that later). Then there's the "centerline," which divides each side's kitchen, making sure you and your partner aren't stepping on each other's toes.

2.2 The Equipment

Paddles

In the world of pickleball, the paddle is an extension of the player. While earlier versions were wooden and basic, modern paddles have evolved into advanced tools crafted from composite materials, such as carbon fiber. They now cater to every style of play, whether you're looking to slam with power or finesse your way to victory. Some people believe that the more expensive the paddle, the better they play, but this is debatable. It's important to remember that it's not about the price or size of your paddle, but how you use it.

Pickleball Aim Trainers

Pickleball aim trainers, also known as target training paddles, are specialized tools designed to help players improve their accuracy and control. These paddles are much smaller than traditional pickleball paddles, which forces players to focus on hitting the ball with the sweet spot—the center of the paddle. By practicing with a smaller surface area, players can develop better precision and consistency, making them more effective during actual game-play. Aim trainers are particularly useful for beginners learning to hit consistently or for more advanced players looking to fine-tune their control.

Balls

The pickleball is not just any plastic ball with holes; it has been uniquely crafted for the sport. While it may look somewhat like a wiffle ball, it is not one—so avoid the mistake of calling it that, or you might get the stink eye from your fellow pickleball enthusiasts! Pickleballs are specially de-signed for the sport of—yes, you guessed it—pickleball, and they come in different sizes, weights, and hole patterns. The type of ball you use—whether for indoor or outdoor play—can significantly affect your game. Learning to master the nuances of each type of pickleball is a skill in itself.

Net

A constant in every game, the net stands proud at 36 inches on the sides, subtly dipping to 34 inches at the center—kind of like a graceful slouch after a long day of keeping rallies in check. It's more than just a barrier; it's the ultimate judge, deciding who wins the battle of finesse and who sends their shot to the land of "almost." Players might curse its existence when their best shot gets rejected (or even lament that the net jumped up to stop them), but deep down, we all know the net is just doing its job—one missed dink at a time.

2.3 Rules of the Game

Scoring

Navigating pickleball scoring can feel like learning an entirely new dialect, but with a touch of patience and a sprinkle of practice, you'll soon be fluent. The beauty of pickleball lies in its unique scoring system, setting it apart from other racket sports. Whether you're diving into a singles match or teaming up for doubles, understanding this system is key to conquering the court.

General Scoring Principles

In pickleball, only the serving team or player has the privilege of earning points. That's right—if you're not serving, you're just playing defense! The standard objective is to reach 11 points in a regular game, though some games or tournaments may be played to 15 or 21 points, especially in longer formats like doubles or championship matches. But don't start celebrating too early; victory doesn't come easy. To claim the win, you must lead by at least two points. So, even if you're at 10-10 or 20-20, prepare to keep battling until someone pulls ahead by two. And remember— pickleball thrives on drama! You might just find yourself in nail-biting rallies, making that final two-point lead feel like you're fighting for the last cookie on a plate. Just when you think it's yours, someone swoops in with a perfect shot, and you're left with crumbs (aka a bruised ego).

The Three-Part Score Announcement

Especially in doubles, it's essential to keep track of the score and who's serving. When announcing the score, you'll state three numbers in quick succession:

- The serving team's current score.
- The receiving team's score.
- The server number (either 1 or 2) – vital in doubles to distinguish between partners.
- For instance, "6-4-2" means the serving team has 6 points, the receiving team 4 points, and the second partner of the serving team is about to serve.

Starting Off as 0-0-2 in Doubles

Now, here's a quirk that often leaves new-comers scratching their heads: when starting a doubles match, the score begins as "0-0-2," which means:

- **0:** Serving team's score.

- **0:** Receiving team's score.
- **2:** Indicates the second server. At the start of the game, only one player serves, so it starts with the "second" server by convention.

After the first server loses the rally, the other team gets the serve, and the score resets to "0-0-1," meaning:

- **0:** Serving team's score (now the new serving team).
- **0:** Receiving team's score.
- **1:** Indicates the first server of the new team is serving.

In pickleball doubles, each team has two servers per turn (except at the start). After both servers lose the rally, the serve switches to the other team. This peculiar start of 0-0-2 in pickleball ensures that both teams get an equal opportunity to serve before points begin to tally up. After this initial serve, the serve passes to the opposing team, and from there, the typical sequence of serving (1 then 2) takes place.

Scoring in Singles

The spirit of the scoring system remains consistent in singles: only the server can notch up those precious points. However, without a partner, there's no need to announce a "server number." Instead, a server in singles will announce just two numbers: their score followed by the opponent's score. A call of "4-2" indicates the server has 4 points while their opponent sits at 2.

Switching Sides

The pickleball court isn't merely a stage for showcasing athletic prowess; it's a battle-ground of strategy. Changing sides not only ensures fairness but also forces players to adapt to varying conditions. Factors such as sun, wind direction, shadows, or even background distractions can play a significant role in a match. By switching sides (optional, and only if everyone agrees), the game ensures that no player or team has a prolonged advantage due to these external variables.

- In games played to 11 points, players swap sides when one team reaches 6 points.
- In 15-point games, players switch sides when one team accumulates 8 points.
- For 21-point matches, players change ends when one team achieves 11 points.

Optional Side Switching

Players also have the option to switch sides after each game, or at agreed-upon intervals during the game, but this is entirely optional and negotiable among all players. If all players agree, switching sides can happen after any game, adding flexibility to accommodate player preferences.

Remember, the player or team that was about to serve before the side change will continue to serve after switching sides.

Pickleball's scoring system, with its intricacies and nuances, adds a layer of strategic depth to the sport. By mastering this dialect, you'll not only keep up with the pace of the game but also gain a psychological edge, as you confidently call out scores and strategize your way to victory.

Playing Singles Across One Section of the Court

When you're playing singles but want to limit the action to one section of the court, the game becomes more about precision, control, and positioning. Instead of using the full width of the pickleball court, players focus on keeping the ball within one half, creating a fast-paced game that sharpens your angles and accuracy.

Here's how to play:

1. **Set Up Boundaries:** Instead of playing across the entire width of the court, pick one half (either the left or right side) to play on. You can stick to one section for the entire game or alternate between sides, just like you would in a doubles game. This adds variety and keeps the challenge fresh.

2. **The Serve:** Serves must be directed into the opposing player's service box on the chosen half. The same serving rules apply as in traditional singles,

except the ball must stay within that section of the court.

3. **Game Play:** All volleys, returns, and shots must land within the designated half of the court. You can decide whether to stick to one side for the whole game or switch sides every few points to keep both players on their toes. If a player hits outside of the chosen section, it's considered out of bounds, and the other player scores or gains the serve.

4. **Scoring:** Play can follow traditional pickleball singles scoring (only the serving player can score points), or you can adapt the rules based on your preferences or to increase competitiveness.

Playing with Three People: Rotational Singles or Two-on-One

When you only have three players, you can still enjoy the same format by rotating positions between points, or for an added challenge, two players can team up against one, with all shots restricted to a single section of the court.

Here's how to play:

1. **Set the Court:** As in the two-person format, use only one half of the court. You can either rotate players after each point or have two players face off against one. The catch? The two players can only hit into the designated box (one half of the court) just like in a normal singles game.

2. **Two-on-One Play:** If you're playing two against one, the two players can use the entire half-court but must direct all shots into the smaller target area—the designated box on the opponent's side. The single player only needs to defend that section, making it a great test of precision and strategy.

3. **Player Rotation:** In the standard rotational game, the two players on court face off, while the third player waits behind the baseline of the receiving side. After each point, the waiting player rotates in, replacing the server, while the server rotates out. In the

two-on-one version, you can switch who is playing solo every few points to give everyone a turn defending the smaller court.

4. **Serve and Scoring:** Follow normal serving and scoring rules, keeping the play restricted to the designated section. In two-on-one games, you can decide whether the team of two or the solo player has the exclusive right to score, or you can allow scoring for either side, depending on the difficulty level you want to create.

5. **Switching Sides:** Just like in doubles, you can alternate sides between sets or every few points to make the game more dynamic and allow each player to experience different angles and challenges.

6. **Continuous Play:** Whether you're rotating positions or playing two-on-one, everyone stays engaged. This format is perfect for practicing accuracy, control, and defensive tactics while ensuring no one sits on the sidelines for too long.

Serving

Mastering the serve in pickleball is akin to perfecting the opening move in a game of chess. It sets the tone, provides an advantage, and can be the difference between seizing or ceding control of the rally.

The Mechanics

The serve in pickleball is uniquely underhand. This isn't your typical tennis or badminton overhead slam. The arm must move in an upward arc, and the paddle contact with the ball should be below the navel. But just because it's underhand doesn't mean it lacks power or precision!

The Destination

Your serve must cross the court diagonally, ensuring it lands within the boundaries of the opponent's service court. While you're aiming, there's a "no-fly zone" you must avoid: the seven-foot non-volley zone, fondly nicknamed the "kitchen." Serving into the kitchen? That's a recipe for handing your opponents an advantage.

Footwork Fundamentals

You might be thinking, "It's just serving, how complicated can the footwork be?" The answer: more than you'd expect! When you serve, both feet must stay behind the baseline. Step on or over it before making contact with the ball, and you've just gifted your opponent a point. Additionally, keep your weight balanced on the balls of your feet to ensure quick lateral movement. Try to stay on both feet and not get off balance as playing on one foot (no matter how gracefully "ballet" it may look) can be a recipe for injuries! Practicing good footwork will ensure that you're poised and grounded as you unleash your serve.

Faults

Ah, faults. Every pickleball player, from fresh beginners to seasoned pros, has encountered them. Think of faults as those uninvited guests that sometimes crash the party. While they're part of the game, knowing them inside out helps in minimizing their appearances.

Boundary Blunders

The court has clearly marked lines for a reason. Hitting the ball outside these boundaries? That's a fault. While those line-skimming shots can be tempting, they come with a risk.

Kitchen Catastrophes

The "kitchen" or the non-volley zone is a unique feature of pickleball. Stepping into the kitchen while volleying the ball (hitting it before it bounces) is a big no-no. It's a fault that can quickly turn the tide of a rally. So, while the kitchen may beckon, remember: no volleying allowed!

Net Nuisances

The net is that ever-present barrier in your quest for scoring. A ball that doesn't clear the net or touches the net during service is considered a fault. Ensure your serves and returns have enough height to gracefully sail over but not too much to go astray.

Post-Fault Proceedings

Faults aren't just minor hiccups; they carry consequences. After a fault, the serving right either shifts to the opponent (in singles) or rotates to the partner (in doubles). This rotation ensures everyone gets a fair chance to serve and keeps the game's rhythm flowing.

Errors and faults might seem daunting, but they're also learning opportunities. As a pro, I've had my fair share of faults and used each one as a stepping stone towards refining my game. Embrace them, learn from them, and let them guide your path to pickleball excellence!

CHAPTER 3

Getting Started

3.1 Choosing the Right Equipment

Paddles: The Power Behind Every Stroke

Ah, the paddle – your weapon of choice on the pickleball court. It's more than just a piece of equipment; it's an extension of you, your style, and your strategy.

The Weight Debate

The question of paddle weight is like asking if you prefer speed or strength. For those nimble-footed players who thrive on quick volleys and precise dinks, a lighter paddle is your best friend. It offers responsiveness and agility. But for those who like to dominate with power-packed smashes, a heavier paddle brings the thunder. It's all about finding the balance that complements your playstyle.

Grip Matters

Never underestimate the importance of a good grip. A handle that's too large can strain your wrist; one that's too small can slip from your hand in the heat of a rally. The right grip ensures optimal control and minimizes injury risk. Your hand should comfortably wrap around the handle, allowing for slight spacing between fingers.

Balls: More Than Just a Color Choice

Pickleball is as much a game of skill as it is a game of equipment choice. And when it comes to equipment, the ball holds significant importance. It's not just a simple matter of color preference; there's science and strategy involved in your choice.

Design Matters

Each pickleball is designed with a specific purpose in mind. They may all look similar at first glance, but a closer look reveals variations in size, weight, and number of holes. These differences influence how the ball travels through the air, how it bounces, and how it reacts upon impact with the paddle.

- *Number of Holes:* Balls can have anywhere from 26 to 40 holes. The number and arrangement of these holes can impact the ball's flight path and its resistance to wind.

- *Surface Texture:* Some balls have a rougher surface, while others are quite smooth. A rougher surface can create more drag, affecting the speed and direction of the ball.

Weighty Decisions

The weight of a pickleball plays a critical role in its behavior during play. Heavier balls tend to travel in a more predictable manner, especially in windy conditions. They also tend to bounce lower, requiring players to adjust their playing techniques. Lighter balls, on the other hand, can be quicker and bounce higher, but they're also more susceptible to being affected by environmental conditions.

Environment Specifics

- Outdoor Play: Outdoor conditions introduce unpredictability, especially if it's windy. Here, you'll benefit from a heavier ball with smaller holes. Such balls are less prone to veering off course in the wind, giving you more control over your shots.

- Indoor Play: Without the interference of wind, indoor play offers more consistency in conditions. A lighter ball with larger holes is preferable here. It allows for a different kind of game, with longer rallies and more room for strategic shot placements.

Durable and Visible

Beyond the technical aspects, durability is a vital factor. Frequent play can wear down a ball, so always opt for ones known for their longevity. Additionally, while color might seem like a mere aesthetic choice, it can affect visibility. Brighter colors, like neon or optic yellow, can be easier to spot in various lighting conditions, giving you a split-second advantage in reaction time.

The choice of a pickleball can profoundly impact your game. Whether you're a novice getting a feel for the sport or a seasoned pro refining your strategy, understanding the nuances of ball selection can give you a competitive edge. So the next time you're faced with a myriad of balls, remember: it's more than just a color choice.

Footwear and Attire: Dressing the Part

Looking good on the court is a bonus, but feeling good? That's essential.

Every sport has its specific nuances when it comes to equipment and attire, and pickleball is no exception. To maximize performance and reduce the risk of injury, it's essential to wear the right gear. Plus, being dressed appropriately boosts confidence and, let's admit it, style points on the court!

Shoe Selection

While you might be tempted to throw on those old tennis shoes, consider this: pickleball-specific shoes are crafted for the game. They offer superior grip, ensuring you don't slip during those intense rallies, and enhanced support, perfect for those quick lateral movements.

The importance of choosing the right shoe for pickleball cannot be overstated.

- **Grip and Safety:** Pickleball-specific shoes have a sole design that caters to the quick starts, stops, and side-to-side movements inherent in the sport. This ensures you maintain traction and reduces the risk of slips and falls.

- **Support and Comfort:** These shoes also come with reinforced sides for lateral support and cushioned insoles for comfort. Given the nature of pickleball's play, where quick reflexes and agility are key, these features can significantly enhance your on-court experience.

Attire Essentials

Your clothes should work with you, not against you. The right choice can make a noticeable difference in your agility, comfort, and overall performance.

- **Material Matters:** Look for garments made from breathable and moisture-wicking materials. This helps regulate body temperature and keeps sweat at bay, ensuring you remain cool and dry throughout the match.

- **Fit is Key:** While some players prefer loose-fitting attire for comfort, it's crucial to ensure that clothing doesn't restrict movement or become a hindrance during play. Consider apparel that offers a balance between ease of movement and a snug fit.

Shading and Sun Protection

Playing outdoors brings an additional set of challenges: sun exposure.

- **Hats and Visors:** A hat or visor is more than just a fashion statement in pickleball. It serves the crucial purpose of shading your eyes from direct sunlight, improving visibility. The brim of a good pickleball hat or visor is designed to provide shade without obstructing peripheral vision—a key factor during those rapid exchanges at the net.

- **Sunscreen:** Protecting your skin from harmful UV rays is paramount. Always apply a sport-specific sunscreen to exposed areas, especially if you're playing during peak sun hours. This not only protects against potential sunburn but also long-term skin damage.

Remember, each piece of gear you choose contributes to your overall playing experience. Whether you're starting out or pushing professional boundaries, never underestimate the combined power of appropriate footwear and attire. Because in pickleball, as in life, the right choices can set you up for success.

3.2 Where to Play: Courts and Venues

Ah, the battlefield! Deciding where to play is just as essential as knowing how to play. There's a certain thrill in exploring different venues, each offering a unique playing experience. Let's dive into your options:

Public Parks

These remain the go-to for most players, especially those just starting out. They're accessible, often free, and give you that fresh, open-air ambiance. But do keep in mind that, while they're convenient, they can also get crowded, especially on weekends or during peak hours. Early mornings or late afternoons might offer a quieter experience.

Sports Clubs

For those looking to add a touch of luxury to their pickleball escapades, sports clubs are the way to go. Premium courts with cushioned surfaces make for a comfortable play, and those night lights? A game-changer for evening matches. Clubs may also offer additional amenities like locker rooms, refreshment areas, and professional coaching.

Indoor Courts

Rain, shine, or snow – indoor courts ensure your game isn't at the mercy of the elements. Apart from weather protection, these courts often have consistent lighting, ensuring visibility remains top-notch throughout your game. However, do note that indoor venues can sometimes have different acoustics, which might slightly alter the sound of your play.

DIY Courts

If you've got space, why not? Transform your driveway or backyard into your personal pickleball haven. The advantage? You get to play whenever you want! But, setting it up requires some investment in equipment and, possibly, surface leveling.

Navigating the Pickleball "Sound" Dilemma

Now, here's a note on a somewhat unexpected challenge: the sound of pickleball. Some find the rhythmic pop-pop-pop of the ball therapeutic, while others, well, not so much. In densely populated areas or neighborhoods that prioritize tranquility, the sound can be a bone of contention.

If you find yourself faced with noise concerns:

- *Paddle and Ball Choice:* Opt for quieter paddles and balls. Some brands specifically design equipment to reduce noise.

- *Portable Sound Barriers:* Consider setting up temporary sound barriers around the court. Acoustic screens or panels can dampen the noise, making it more neighborhood-friendly.

- *Play Hours:* Respect community quiet hours. Avoid early morning or late-night sessions in residential areas.

- *Community Engagement:* Organize community awareness sessions or introductory workshops. Sometimes, understanding and experiencing the game firsthand can turn critics into fans!

- *Seek Alternatives:* If the noise remains an unresolved issue, consider relocating to a more isolated area or explore indoor venues.

In short, your playing venue can significantly impact your pickleball experience. Whether it's the ambiance, the court surface, or the community dynamics, choose a place that complements your game style and respects the environment around you.

3.3 Pre-game Warm-up, Safety, and Vision Protection

Okay, let's get something straight. You wouldn't start your car on a frosty morning without letting it warm up a bit, right? Same principle applies to your body before a game of pickleball. Proper preparation is key, and that means more than just grabbing a paddle.

Step 1: Ignite Those Muscles!

Begin with 5-10 minutes of light jogging around the court. This not only gets your heart rate up but also preps your muscles for the action ahead. Next, add some dynamic stretches, think leg swings, arm circles, and gentle torso rotations. These moves will give you a good range of motion and help prevent those pesky injuries. Now, once you're warmed up, engage in easy rallies with your partner to get a feel for the ball and the court.

Step 2: Gear Up for Safety

While pickleball might seem like a gentler sport compared to, say, rugby, injuries can happen, especially if you're the sort to give it your all. Do you dive for those almost-out-of-reach shots? Consider strapping on knee and elbow pads. A scraped elbow or knee isn't a badge of honor; it's a sign you could've been better prepared!

Step 3: Protect Those Peepers!

You've got the basics down, but there's another essential piece of gear you might be overlooking: safety goggles. Now, if you're playing outdoors on a blazing sunny day, a good pair of UV-protective sunglasses is your best friend. But here's the deal for those who've had LASIK surgery or just want an extra layer of eye protection – safety goggles can be a game changer. They shield your eyes from unexpected ball bounces or errant paddle swings. And if you're thinking, "Goggles? On a pickleball court?", trust me, it's better to be the player with goggles than the one wishing they'd worn them after an unfortunate incident.

In a nutshell? Warm up, gear up, and never underestimate the importance of keeping those eyes safe. With preparation and the right gear, you're setting yourself up not only for a winning game but for many more games in the future.

3.4 Basic Grip Techniques

Let's put it in simple terms: the way you grip your pickleball paddle is akin to how a writer holds their pen. It's foundational, dictating every move and stroke you make on the court.

The Continental Grip: The All-Purpose Tool

Often dubbed the Swiss Army knife of grips, the Continental is your go-to for versatility. Perfect for those transitioning between forehand and backhand shots, its mechanics are straightforward: imagine holding a hammer, and that's how your hand should wrap around the paddle. Simple in concept, but mighty in execution.

The Eastern Grip: For the Forehand Enthusiast

Craving a bit more force in your forehand shots? The Eastern Grip is your answer. Starting from the Continental grip, rotate your paddle slightly anticlockwise. You'll see your knuckles aiming more towards the heavens. While it might offer a smidgen less in wrist flexibility, it compensates with a powerful punch for those assertive forehand drives.

Beyond the Basics: Exploring Other Grips (Not Recommended)

While the Continental and Eastern grips are the gold standard in pickleball, players transitioning from other racquet sports sometimes bring in alternative grips. These grips, although effective in their original sports, can form bad habits in pickleball. Here are a few of those grips:

- *Western Grip:* A deeper grip where the base knuckle of the index finger rests on the bottom plane of the paddle handle. While it allows for extreme topspin in tennis, its adaptability in pickleball is limited, making quick transitions between different shots a challenge.

- *Finger-Up Grip:* Here, the index finger extends up onto the back of the paddle face. Originally from table tennis, it offers players a heightened touch and can provide an enhanced sense of direction. However, potential strain risks and reduced stability make it less favored for intense pickleball plays.

- *Pistol Grip:* Held more with the fingertips than deep in the palm, this grip enhances wrist flexibility, appealing to players who favor 'snap' in their shots. However, it can compromise the stability required for powerful pickleball shots.

- *Double-handed Backhand:* Involving both hands on the paddle, much like a two-handed tennis backhand, it provides added power and stability for backhand shots. However, its reduced reach is a clear disadvantage in pickleball's wide-ranging court dynamics.

Final Thoughts on Grip

Regardless of whether you're stepping onto the pickleball court for the first time or returning as an old hand, your grip remains paramount. It's the handshake between your paddle and the ball, molding power, precision, and style. Whether you're a newcomer hunting foundational wisdom or a veteran revisiting core principles, always remember: your grip is where the journey begins.

Remember, you're not merely holding a paddle; you're brandishing an instrument forged for victory.

CHAPTER 4

Basic Skills and Techniques

4.1 The Serve

Let's start at square one—or rather, square seven (feet behind the net, that is!). The serve sets the stage for every point, so it's crucial to get it right.

Underhand Serve

Unlike tennis, pickleball serves are underhand. Your paddle must be below your wrist and the ball below your waist when making contact. The key is to swing from low to high, ensuring that the ball arcs gently over the net and into the opponent's service square.

Launching the game with a stellar serve isn't just about style; it's about strategy. Understanding the dynamics of an effective serve can be the difference between an easy point and a challenging rally.

Power vs. Placement: The Eternal Debate

Unleashing a powerful serve can feel exhilarating, but smart players recognize that accuracy often outweighs sheer force. Instead of aiming for sonic speed, consider placing your serves strategically. Targeting corners or changing up the serve's depth can disrupt your opponent's rhythm, paving the way for a favorable rally.

4.2 The Return

Returning a serve isn't merely about keeping the ball in play; it's about laying down the groundwork for a winning point.

Deep Returns

The aim is to hit the ball deep into your opponent's court. A deep return pushes them back, giving you time to advance and take control of the court.

Footwork

Don't just stand there like a statue waiting for the ball to come to you! Stay alert, watch your opponent's body language, and anticipate their next move. Keep a slight bend in your knees and be ready to move laterally or forward to meet the ball. Anticipation is key; reacting alone won't cut it. Agile footwork is crucial in order to dominate. Remember, each serve and return is a golden opportunity to dictate the game's tempo.

4.3 The Dink

The dink is the pickleball equivalent of a mic drop. It's a soft shot, aimed just over the net, designed to mess with players who are better at power shots than finesse.

When to Dink

Usually, you'll dink when both you and your opponent are up at the net. It's the ideal counterpunch when you're locked in a "kitchen" face-off.

The Technique

Open the paddle face slightly, and use a relaxed grip to gently push the ball so it arcs over the net, ideally landing in the opponent's kitchen. It's all wrist control and touch.

4.4 The Lob

Ah, the lob—a rainbow arcing over the battlefield!

The lob, when executed correctly, can be one of the most effective shots in your pickleball arsenal. Done wrong, it's a gift to your opponents. Done right, it can turn the tide of a game.

Defensive vs. Offensive Lobs

- *Defensive Lob:* When you find yourself out of position or under pressure, a defensive lob can be your best friend. The main purpose here is to give yourself and your partner time to reset and get back into a better position. Ideally, a defensive lob should be high enough to push the opponents back, making it difficult for them to smash it down with power. Your goal isn't necessarily to win the point outright with this shot but to regain control of the rally.

- *Offensive Lob:* The offensive lob is more than just a shot to buy time—it's a tactical decision. When you notice your opponents are too close to the net or are anticipating a dink or drive, a well-placed offensive lob can catch them off-guard. The key here is precision. If it's too short, it's an easy overhead smash for them. Too long, and it's out. But hit just right, it can force your opponents into a scramble, often resulting in a weak return or no return at all.

Execution

1. Grip and Stance
- Use a continental grip or slightly modified eastern grip for better paddle face control.
- Set your feet shoulder-width apart with knees slightly bent.

2. Preparation
- As with all shots in pickleball, preparation is key. Before striking, rotate your shoulders and hips slightly, transferring weight to your back foot.
- Keep your eye on the ball and be prepared to adjust based on its speed and trajectory.

3. Stroke and Follow-Through

- Contact the ball below waist level and use an upward motion to send it high.
- The paddle face should be open, aiming to make contact with the ball's lower half.
- Follow through with your stroke, finishing high to ensure a good arc.

4. Placement

- Your target is over the opponents but within the boundaries of the court.
- Remember to factor in elements like wind if you're playing outdoors. Wind can drastically change the ball's path. If you're playing into the wind, you may need to hit a bit harder than usual. If it's behind you, a gentler touch might be needed.

5. Adjustment

- Not every lob will be perfect, and that's okay. Always be prepared to move and adjust your position after you've hit a lob, anticipating your opponents' next shot.

In conclusion, mastering the lob can add a new dimension to your game. By knowing when and how to use both defensive and offensive lobs, you'll keep your opponents guessing and gain a strategic advantage. Remember, practice makes perfect, so spend time refining your lob on the court to make it a reliable part of your pickleball toolkit.

4.5 Groundstrokes

Groundstrokes are foundational in pickleball, just as they are in any racquet sport. Being proficient in these baseline shots is essential, as they set up your approach to the net, where much of the action in pickleball occurs.

Forehand and Backhand

Forehand

- **Grip and Stance:** Adopt a semi-western grip or eastern grip. Position your feet roughly shoulder-width apart, with your weight balanced on the balls of your feet.

- **Swing Path:** Start with your paddle back, rotate your hips and shoulders, then swing forward, making contact with the ball in front of you.
- **Follow Through:** Ensure a smooth follow-through, extending your paddle towards your target. This not only guides the ball but also reduces the risk of injuries.

Backhand

- **Grip and Stance:** A continental or eastern backhand grip works best. Again, maintain a shoulder-width stance and stay on the balls of your feet.
- **Swing Path:** Rotate your hips and shoulders as you pull the paddle back. Strike the ball in front and slightly to the side of your body.
- **Follow Through:** The paddle should finish high, with the tip pointing towards the intended direction.

With practice, the backhand will become just as formidable as the forehand, allowing you to cover the court more efficiently and fend off targeted shots from opponents.

Spin or No Spin

Topspin

- Use a low-to-high swing path. The objective is to brush the ball with the paddle, creating forward spin. This makes the ball dip quickly after crossing the net, reducing the chance of hitting out.

Slice or Underspin

- This requires a high-to-low swing. By striking the ball with a slightly open paddle face, you create backspin which causes the ball to skid or stay low after the bounce.

Flat

- A flat shot uses a straightforward swing path, with little to no upward or downward motion. It's the most direct and often the fastest groundstroke, but with less margin for error over the net.

Incorporating spins can keep your opponent off-balance and guessing, while flat shots can be employed for aggressive play and to capitalize on weak returns.

To conclude, groundstrokes form the backbone of your pickleball game. By mastering the forehand and backhand, along with understanding when to use spin, you'll establish a strong base from which to build advanced strategies and techniques. Whether you're just starting out or aiming to be a pro, refining these basic skills is crucial. So get out there, practice, and watch your game soar!

CHAPTER 5

Mastering Advanced Techniques

Pickleball is a sport of depth. The deeper you delve, the more nuances you discover. Whether you're aiming to compete at a higher level or just want to impress your fellow players, mastering advanced techniques will give you that cutting edge. Let's dive in.

5.1 Spin Serve

A spin serve isn't just about deception—it's about laying the groundwork for your subsequent shots. It sets the tone and catches your opponents off-balance.

Types of Spin

- **Topspin:** Imparted by brushing up on the ball, topspin makes the ball dip quickly after clearing the net. This forces your opponent to play upwards, creating an opportunity for you to dictate the next shot.

- **Backspin (Underspin):** Achieved by striking under the ball with a downward motion. Backspin causes the ball to slow down and bounce low, often forcing your opponent to lift the ball on the return.
- **Sidespin:** Achieved by striking the ball sideways, sidespin makes the ball curve unpredictably upon bouncing, throwing off your opponent's rhythm.

Technique Tips

- **Wrist Movement:** A loose wrist is crucial. The flick of the wrist at the point of contact imparts the necessary spin.
- **Contact Point:** For topspin, hit the lower half of the ball; for backspin, contact the bottom of the ball; for sidespin, strike the ball towards the side you want the spin to go.

5.2 Slams and Overheads

Power and precision define these shots. They're about seizing the initiative and establishing dominance.

Positioning and Timing

- **Prepare Early:** Set up for the shot as soon as you see a weak return or a short lob. An early preparation allows for better shot selection.
- **Follow Through:** Extend your arm completely, ensuring maximum power is transferred to the ball.

5.3 The Third Shot Drop

This shot is about control and transitioning from defense to offense. When executed right, it gives you a strategic advantage.

Execution Keys

- **Soft Hands:** Maintain a relaxed grip to allow for better feel and control of the shot.
- **Paddle Angle:** A slightly open paddle face ensures the ball clears the net but drops quickly.

5.4 Defensive Strategies

Every champion knows that offense wins games, but defense wins championships. In pickleball, a solid defense can frustrate opponents and create offensive opportunities.

Essential Defensive Shots

- **The Dig:** When the ball is hit hard at your feet, use a low to high paddle motion to "dig" the ball up and over the net.
- **Lobs:** When under pressure, a well-placed lob can move your opponents back, giving you time to reset.

Mastering these techniques takes time and consistent practice. But once integrated into your gameplay, they can elevate your status from an intermediate player to an advanced tactician. Remember, in pickleball, every shot has a purpose. With these advanced techniques, make every shot count!

CHAPTER 6
Game Strategies

Now it's time to go beyond mere shots and delve into the realms of strategic play and rulebook savvy.

6.1 Singles vs. Doubles: The Court Tango

In the world of pickleball, two distinct dance forms emerge: the solo act of singles and the synchronized choreography of doubles. Dive in to discover their rhythms.

Singles

Ah, singles, the Lone Ranger of pickleball. Here, you're the captain of your ship, charting the waters of the court.

- **Stamina and Coverage:** Flying solo? That means the entire dance floor is yours. Quick footwork and a tactical mind are your tickets to victory. Keep those sneakers moving and eyes peeled!

- **Shot Placement:** Think of it as leading your opponent in a dance. Send them twirling to the left, then spinning to the right. Use crosscourt shots, surprise lobs, and deep drives to keep them on their toes.

- **Psychological Play:** Singles is a mind game. Pay attention! Is your opponent's confidence waning after a missed shot? These tiny cues can craft a playbook to keep them guessing.

Doubles

Welcome to the ensemble performance. Doubles is where teamwork makes the dream work!

- **Communication:** It's the secret sauce. More than just shouting "Yours!" or "Mine!", it's about syncing up like the best of dance partners. Can you predict your partner's next step? That's the goal.

- **Court Dynamics:** Now, there are four of you sharing the spotlight. Recognize your zones and play them to perfection. Don't step on anyone's toes!
- **Serve Rotation:** This isn't a free-for-all; there's a sequence to the spotlight. Get familiar with the serve dance, so there's no mid-game mix-up.
- **Complementary Play:** Know your dance partner's strengths. If they're the Fred Astaire of frontcourt play, let them lead there. Play to your combined strengths and make magic.

Whether it's the solo shuffle of singles or the dynamic duet of doubles, mastering these nuances is your key to pickleball prowess.

6.2 Understanding Your Opponent

Sun Tzu said, "Know your enemy," and indeed, he'd have been quite the pickleball detective. Your opponent holds clues; it's your job to uncover them.

Observation

- **Analyze Serving Patterns:** Is there a favorite serve up their sleeve? Are they favoring spin or power? Become a sleuth and decode their strategies.
- **Footwork and Positioning:** Watch their steps. Are they light on their feet or a tad hesitant in their moves? These can be telling signs.
- **Identify Strengths and Vulnerabilities:** A wobbly backhand? A drop shot that's more tell than show? Every player has a tell-tale sign, and spotting it can be your game-changer.

Adaptation

Alter Your Approach Based on Observations

Net Avoiders

If your opponent is hesitant at the net, use a few drop shots to draw them in. This will expose their weakness. If they are uncomfortable at the net, they are more likely to make errors when forced to play closer to it.

This will also limit their time to react since players who avoid the net generally have more time to react to deep shots. Drawing them closer forces them to play faster and under pressure. Additionally, by pulling them forward, you open up the space behind them for deeper shots, making them scramble and get off-balance.

Baseline Players

If your opponent is staying mostly at the baseline, challenge them with a short serve or a drop shot to force them to move forward. This challenges a baseline player since they are comfortable with long rallies. A short serve or drop shot forces them to move out of their comfort zone and could lead to mistakes. Baseline players also prefer staying back for more time to react. Forcing them to move forward disrupts their rhythm and makes it harder for them to maintain control over the game.

- **Control the Rally:** Set the stage and rhythm. Make them dance to your tune.

6.3 The Importance of Communication in Doubles

In doubles, it's a duet. Like any good duet, you need to be in sync to succeed.

The Callouts

- **Avoiding Overlaps and Collisions:** Call out "yours" or "mine" to prevent confusion. When one player moves up to the net, the other should shift back slightly to cover. Clear communication avoids both players ending up in the same spot.

- **Feedback and Adjustments:** After each point, briefly check in with your partner. If a lob was missed, say, "Let's watch for high shots." If a successful drop shot worked, acknowledge it: "Great drop—keep doing that!" Keep feedback short and actionable to stay focused on the game.

- **Positive Reinforcement:** A little cheer can go a long way. Keep the vibes upbeat and the spirits high. Don't be a "Negative Nelly" and roll your eyes when your partner misses a shot. Give them encouragement. And definitely don't bark at them and tell them how to play the game better! That's a sure way to not be asked to partner again. Helpful hints are okay, but only if done in a positive way and if your partner is open to feedback. Similarly, don't denigrate yourself if you miss a shot. Positive reinforcement should be given to yourself, as well!

The Strategies

- **Non-verbal Cues:** A quick look, hand signal, or nod can communicate just as effectively as words. Use non-verbal cues to signal positioning changes, poaching, or planned plays without alerting your opponents. For example, a raised paddle could indicate a lob is coming.

- **Defined Roles and Responsibilities:** Know who covers what. One player might focus on covering the net while the other stays back. Decide these roles in advance, and trust your partner to stick to them. For example, if your partner rushes forward, you should automatically move back to balance the court coverage.

6.4 Adapting to Different Playing Styles

Pickleball players come in varied flavors. Knowing how to play against each style? That's your ace.

Speed Demons vs. Strategists

- **Assessing and Countering Pace:** Against a speedster, it's not about matching their speed, but redirecting their shots with control. Use their power against them by aiming for angles. For slower, strategic players, break their rhythm with surprise shots like quick volleys or lobs.
- **Dominating Central Positions:** The court's "T" is the prime spot. Hold your ground there and force your opponent to the sidelines. Controlling this area gives you the advantage in dictating the game's pace.

Changing Gears

- **Adjusting Shot Techniques:** Mix up your shots. If your opponent is anticipating your hard smashes, switch to soft dinks or slices. The constant change in speed and spin will keep them on their toes.

- **Recognizing Mid-Game Changes:** Stay alert. Your opponent's strategy can shift mid-game. Be ready to adjust and respond to their new tactics, whether they increase their pace or start playing more defensively.

In the grand dance of pickleball, these insights are your choreography. Know them, master them, and you'll glide through every game with finesse and flair.

CHAPTER 7

Playing by the Rules

7.1 Commonly Misunderstood Rules

Just because it's fun doesn't mean pickleball is a lawless land.

The Kitchen Rule

- You can't volley a ball while standing in the non-volley zone (also known as "the kitchen"). And no, you can't cheat by jumping out of it while hitting either!

The Double-Bounce Rule

- Each team must play their first shot off the bounce. That means your serve and the opponent's return must both hit the ground before being struck. After the first bounce on each side (serve and return), however, aerial shots are allowed.

Service Rules

- Picture this: You're serving with an underhand motion, paddle below the wrist, making sure the ball is struck below your waist (or navel area, for precision). Now, here's the kicker— both feet must stay firmly planted behind the baseline. No floating feet here! Unlike tennis, where a dramatic leg lift might add flair, in pickleball, both feet need to stay grounded. You can't have one foot in the air, and neither foot can cross the baseline until after you've struck the ball. It's all about keeping things steady and controlled.

7.2 Official vs. Recreational Play

Recreational play is forgiving; you can overlook some minor infractions. But in official games, you've got referees and precise regulations.

Time Warnings

- While a casual game might afford you leisure, official matches run a tight ship. Be punctual with serves and points, or risk the referee's glare.

Scoring

- Consistency is key! Regardless of the play level, always announce scores with your team's score first, followed by the opponent's, and lastly the server number (for doubles aficionados).

Equipment Check

- Not all paddles are created equal. In official tournaments, ensure your gear is up to spec. That vibrant paddle might be fun for Sunday games but might not make the cut in a professional arena.

Strategic Time-Outs

- Pro tip: Use those allocated time-outs wisely in official games. It's not just for catching your breath; it's for strategizing the next killer move.

7.3 Etiquette and Sportsmanship

Your reputation on the court is as essential as your backhand. Good manners make good players, and the last thing you want to do is show up on the court and get stink-eye because people remember your bad behavior. The following are some basics for good sportsmanship:

Respect

- Be the player everyone wants to partner with or compete against. Steer clear of distracting your opponents or reveling in their missteps.

Fair Play

- Integrity is the name of the game. Admit to your foot fouls or kitchen trespasses, especially in friendly recreational matches where there are no referees. And always be fair with line calls, both theirs and yours.

Post-Game Vibes

- Win with grace, lose with dignity. A simple paddle tap and a "Great match!" go a long way in building respect and rapport.

7.4 Handling Disputes

Where competition thrives, disputes are bound to arise. Disagreements are part of any sport, but they don't have to escalate into World War III. Let's resolve them like the pros.

The Rulebook

- The ultimate decider! Have it handy, be it in a digital copy on your phone or a tangible version tucked in your gear bag.

Sportsmanship

- Yes, it's here again because it's that important. Remember, pickleball is a game. Keep the spirit of fun and friendly competition alive, even when disputes arise. After all, life—and sports—are meant to be enjoyed.

With this approach, you're not just mastering the game of pickleball but also the game of respect, strategy, and sportsmanship.

CHAPTER 8

Competitive Play

Let's dig deeper into the competitive layers of pickleball, where the volleys get intense and the strategies complex.

8.1 Local and National Tournaments

Local Scene: The Starting Block

So you've been crowned the champion of your neighborhood barbecue pickleball game. What next? Local tournaments are the first rung of the ladder. These could range from events organized by community centers to county or even state championships.

Different Types

You'll see a variety of events—singles, doubles, mixed doubles, and sometimes, age-specific divisions. This is your chance to dip your toes in the pool and figure out what suits you best.

Prize Incentives

Trophies and medals are often up for grabs, but occasionally you'll find tournaments with cash prizes or sports gear as incentives. It's not just about glory; there's loot, too!

National Stage: The Big Leagues

Ah, the national stage. This is the Wimbledon of pickleball, complete with professional photographers, live-streaming, and maybe even sponsor booths.

Registration and Fees

Participation often requires pre-registration and entry fees. Some tournaments even have qualifying rounds, so don't waltz in expecting automatic entry into the main draw.

Prestige Events

Some prestigious national events are widely considered the crown jewels of the pickleball circuit. Winning or even just participating in these can skyrocket your player ranking and street cred.

8.2 Player Ratings and Rankings

Ratings: Your Pickleball GPA

Ratings are like your pickleball GPA, an indicator of your current form. They range from 1.0 for beginners to 6.0 for professionals.

How to Get Rated

You can start with a self-assessment but formal ratings, usually ranging from events like 'Round Robins' or official USA Pickleball assessments, are more credible and universally accepted.

Why It Matters

Your rating determines who you'll face in tournaments, so a more accurate rating gives you more evenly-matched and satisfying games.

Rankings: The Cream Rises to the Top

While ratings tell you about your skill level, rankings tell you your standing among those in your skill level.

National Rankings

Think of it as the leaderboard of pickleball. USA Pickleball and other bodies maintain these, based on points accumulated through participating and winning in sanctioned events.

Why It's Important

This isn't just about bragging rights; a higher ranking can help you get sponsorships, media coverage, and can even qualify you for elite competitions.

8.3 Preparing for Competitive Play

Mental Prep: The Inner Game

Pickleball isn't just about quick wrists; it's about a quick mind too. Mental strategies like positive self-talk or visualization exercises can set you in the right frame of mind.

Gear Check: Be Your Own Pit Crew

Imagine losing a point because your paddle's grip slipped! Preparing a gear checklist ensures that your game stays uninterrupted. Spare paddles, grips, strings, shoes, and even a snack could be game-changers.

8.4 Tips from a Pro

Technique Tips: A Pro's Secrets

If you've ever watched a pro game, you'll notice their strokes aren't just powerful; they're precise. Many pros emphasize the importance of shot placement over power.

Advanced Techniques

From spin serves to deceptive volleys, pros often have a range of advanced techniques that they employ to keep their opponents guessing. Observing these can be an education in itself.

Strategy Wisdom: The Third Shot and Beyond

The third shot often dictates how the rest of the point will unfold. Pros often suggest mastering the third shot drop, a soft shot that lands close to the net, making it difficult for opponents to attack.

Doubles Dynamics

In doubles, pros often work in perfect harmony with their partners, so much so that they seem to share a brain. Communication, both verbal and non-verbal, is their secret weapon for perfect positioning and playmaking.

Now, armed with this comprehensive dive into the competitive realm of pickleball, you're not just playing the game; you're in it to win it!

CHAPTER 9
Health and Fitness

9.1 Nutrition and Hydration

Nutrition: Fueling the Machine
In the world of pickleball, precision, agility, and stamina are your prime assets. But no matter how much you train, your performance can fall short if your nutrition is off-mark. Think of your body as the most finely-tuned sports car. Even the best-engineered car won't perform if filled with the wrong fuel.

The Right Carbs
Carbohydrates are your body's primary energy source during intense physical activity. But not all carbs are created equal.

Complex Carbohydrates

These are your best friends on the court. Foods like brown rice, quinoa, oatmeal, and lentils release energy gradually. This means that instead of getting a quick burst of energy followed by a slump, you get a steady stream of fuel. This steady release keeps you agile and focused throughout the game, ensuring that you don't run out of steam halfway through a match.

Simple Carbohydrates

These can be found in foods like fruits, milk, and some processed sweets. While they provide a quick energy boost, relying solely on them can lead to energy crashes. They're great for a quick pre-game snack to kickstart your energy, but for sustained performance, complex carbs are the way to go.

Protein Power

While carbohydrates fuel your game, protein rebuilds and repairs. Intense training and matches can cause micro-tears in your muscles. Protein helps repair these tears, aiding in muscle recovery and growth.

Sources

Consider the diet of elite athletes like LeBron James, who understands the importance of protein in muscle recovery. Incorporating sources like chicken, turkey, fish, tofu, beans, and Greek yogurt, LeBron ensures his body has what it needs for optimal performance. Emulating such nutrition habits of top-tier athletes can be a game-changer for any pickleball player looking to elevate their game.

Hydration: The Elixir of Life

Dehydration can be a silent performance killer. Even a slight decrease in hydration can impair your reaction times, decision-making abilities, and endurance.

Timing

Hydration isn't something you think about an hour before the game. The process should begin at least 48 hours prior. By consistently hydrating, your body is better prepared to handle the sweat loss during intense matches. Aim for at least 8-10 glasses of water daily, increasing this amount in the days leading up to an important match or during rigorous training sessions.

Sports Drinks vs. Water

Pure, simple water is the most straightforward hydration source. But during extended play, especially in hot and humid conditions, you not only lose water but also essential electrolytes like sodium and potassium.

Sports Drinks

These come packed with the necessary electrolytes and can be beneficial in replenishing what you lose during intense matches. They help maintain the body's electrolyte balance, ensuring that muscle cramps and fatigue are kept at bay.

However, it's crucial to choose wisely. Some sports drinks contain excessive sugars which can lead to unnecessary calorie intake. Look for those with lower sugar content or opt for electrolyte tablets that can be added to water.

In conclusion, think of nutrition and hydration as the backstage crew of your pickleball performance. They might not be in the limelight, but without them, the show can't go on. Prioritize them, and watch your game reach new heights.

9.2 Conditioning Exercises

Cardio: The Stamina Factory

Endurance is a crucial component in the fast-paced game of pickleball. A powerful cardiovascular system ensures that you remain alert and active throughout extended rallies, preventing you from becoming the weak link in an intense match.

Cardio Options

- **Running:** This age-old exercise boosts heart health and increases lung capacity. Incorporating regular runs, be it short sprints or long jogs, can significantly benefit your on-court performance.

- **Cycling:** This low-impact exercise strengthens the legs while providing an excellent cardiovascular workout. Plus, cycling can be a fun way to explore your surroundings.

- **On-Court Drills:** These can be tailored to pickleball specifically. Try fast-paced drills, moving side to side, or charging to the net and back. This not only works your cardiovascular system but also hones your on-court skills.

Interval Training

Pickleball isn't a constant-paced game. It's a combination of calm moments and explosive movements. Interval training closely mirrors this rhythm. By alternating between high-intensity exercises and short rest periods, you can enhance your agility and quick recovery.

Practical Exercises

- **Sprint Intervals:** Sprint for 30 seconds, then walk or jog for a minute.

Repeat. This will condition your body for those rapid pickleball rallies.

- **Jump Rope Intervals:** Jump rapidly for a minute, rest for 30 seconds, and then repeat. This improves footwork, vital for pickleball.

Strength Training: Muscle Up

A good shot isn't just about technique; it's about power. And while pickleball may not demand the same muscle mass as weight-lifting, having a strong physical foundation can drastically improve your game.

Effective Workouts

- **Dumbbell Exercises:** Incorporate moves like bicep curls, tricep extensions, and shoulder presses to build arm strength.
- **Leg Workouts:** Squats, lunges, and calf raises can fortify your legs, giving you both stability and strength.

Core Strength

In pickleball, the core is more than just a set of good-looking abs; it's the powerhouse. A robust core offers better balance, more potent shots, and a more excellent range of motion.

Core Workouts

- **Planks:** The gold standard for core conditioning. Whether side, forearm, or straight-arm planks, regularly incorporating them can make a noticeable difference.
- **Russian Twists:** Sitting on the floor, hold a weight with both hands, lean back slightly, and rotate the weight side to side. This works both your obliques and abdominal muscles.
- **Leg Raises:** Lying flat on your back, raise your legs up and down without letting them touch the ground. This targets the lower abs, an often-neglected area.

Incorporate these exercises into your weekly routine, and you'll find yourself more prepared, more powerful, and more poised on the pickleball court. Remember, conditioning is an investment in your game.

Every drop of sweat off-court translates to a better performance on-court.

9.3 Injury Prevention

Warm-Up: The Prelude

Just as a musician doesn't dive into a performance without tuning their instrument, a pickleball player shouldn't jump into a game cold. Warming up is essential to prevent injuries, increase blood flow, and mentally prepare for the game ahead.

Types of Warm-Ups

- **Dynamic Stretches:** These are movements that prepare the muscles you'll use during the game. Leg swings work on hip flexibility, arm circles warm up the shoulders, and jogging laps around the court gets your heart rate up and prepares your body for the pickleball action.
- **Sport-Specific Drills:** These are exercises tailored specifically for pickleball. Practice your swings, volleys, and

serves at a slower pace to prepare both your body and mind.

Protective Gear: Your Armor

Even the most skilled players aren't immune to injuries. Proper protective gear can significantly reduce the risk of sustaining an injury during play.

- **Knee and Elbow Pads:** Especially useful for those who dive or throw themselves into the game, literally. They cushion your joints from impact.
- **Wristbands:** These can help absorb sweat, ensuring your grip remains secure throughout the match.
- **Quality Footwear:** This is non-negotiable. Your shoes are the foundation upon which you play.

The Right Shoes

Investing in the right footwear can make all the difference between a game-winning shot and an injury. Pickleball shoes are designed to support the unique movements of the sport.

- **Grip and Traction:** Specific pickleball shoes have soles designed to grip the court surface, reducing the risk of slips and falls.

- **Ankle Support:** Ankle rolls or twists can be nasty. Shoes with proper ankle support help in preventing such injuries.

9.4 Recovery and Rest

Sleep: The Recovery Room

Rest isn't just the absence of activity; it's a proactive step towards better performance. Sleep is your body's natural mechanism for recovery, healing, and mental clarity.

- **Deep Sleep Phases:** It's not just about the quantity but the quality of sleep. During deep sleep, your body undergoes reparative processes, rebuilding muscles, consolidating memory, and more. Investing in a comfortable mattress, maintaining a consistent sleep schedule, and avoiding screens before bed can promote deeper sleep.

Rest Days: The Unspoken Hero

Rest days are as much a part of training as the actual training itself. While it might seem counterintuitive, muscles grow and strengthen during rest, not during workouts.

- **Active Recovery:** Rest doesn't always mean complete stillness. Activities like yoga provide stretching and relaxation, aiding in muscle recovery without being strenuous. Light swimming is another low-impact exercise that can keep your cardiovascular system active without overburdening the muscles.

In the realm of pickleball, the player is the most prized instrument. By understanding the need for warm-ups, protection, recovery, and rest, you can ensure that this instrument—your body and mind—remains in peak condition, ready to tackle any challenge the court throws at you.

CHAPTER 10
The Social Aspect of Pickleball

10.1 Pickleball Communities

The Bonds of Pickleball

Pickleball's meteoric rise isn't just due to its engaging gameplay but also its inherent nature of fostering community spirit. Unlike many other sports, pickleball uniquely merges diverse age groups and skill levels, creating an environment ripe for forging friendships and building strong bonds.

Where Communities Thrive

- **Retirement Communities:** Many active adult communities have recognized the allure of pickleball, with courts popping up across the nation. These communities often host regular tournaments, providing a fun and active way for seniors to socialize.

- **Colleges and Universities:** The younger generation is catching the pickleball bug, too. Intramural leagues on college campuses are introducing students to the joys of the game, promoting both physical fitness and camaraderie.

- **Local Sports Clubs:** From YMCA to specialized pickleball clubs, local establishments are offering courses, leagues, and open play days dedicated to the sport, making it accessible for everyone.

Online and Offline Groups

Digital age meets age-old love for community. There are numerous online forums, social media groups, and dedicated websites where enthusiasts discuss strategies, share experiences, and even organize local meet-ups.

10.2 Making It a Family Affair

The All-Inclusive Game

Pickleball's beauty lies in its simplicity and inclusivity. The easy-to-grasp rules and lesser physical demands compared to other racquet sports mean that players of varying ages and skill levels can enjoy it together.

Building Bonds on the Court

Playing pickleball with family can serve as a unique bonding experience. It encourages communication, teamwork, and healthy competition, creating lasting memories and strengthening familial ties. And who knows? Sunday family dinners might just transition into Sunday family pickleball tournaments.

10.3 Pickleball and Networking

The New Social Sport

While golf has traditionally been the go-to sport for business networking, pickleball is quickly making its mark. Its relaxed yet engaging nature provides an excellent backdrop for both casual and strategic business conversations.

Business on the Court

Professional pickleball leagues and tournaments are not just about showcasing talent; they're networking goldmines. Entrepreneurs, professionals, and enthusiasts converge, discussing everything from game strategies to business ventures. So, the next time you pack your paddle, consider slipping in a few business cards, too.

10.4 Charitable Events and Fundraisers

Playing with Purpose

Pickleball's rising popularity is being harnessed for the greater good. Numerous events now integrate philanthropy with the sport, making each serve, volley, and smash count for a cause.

Fundraisers and Philanthropy

From local charity drives to larger "Pickleball for a Purpose" events, the community is leveraging the sport's appeal to raise funds and awareness for various causes. Whether it's for health research, community development, or educational programs, pickleball enthusiasts are rallying together to make a difference.

In essence, pickleball is more than just a sport; it's a movement. A movement that's building communities, strengthening families, forging professional ties, and making the world a better place, one game at a time. Join the movement, and discover the myriad ways pickleball can enrich your life.

CHAPTER 11

Music and Pickleball Go Hand in Hand

There's something about pickleball that just begs for a soundtrack. Maybe it's the rhythmic "pop" of the ball against the paddle, or maybe it's the way the game gets you moving. Whatever it is, pickleball and music have a natural chemistry, like peanut butter and jelly—or better yet, dinks and smashes!

11.1 Pickleball's Beat: Why Music Matters

Music isn't just background noise—it's a mood-setter, a pace-setter, and sometimes, your secret weapon for getting into the groove. Whether you're jamming to pop hits, old-school rock, or a funky mix of genres, the right playlist can elevate your pickleball game to new heights.

- **Boosts Energy:** Let's face it, sometimes your energy might be dipping halfway through a match. That's where a great song with an upbeat tempo comes in to save the day. Just when you're thinking you've got nothing left, a solid track will pump you up, keep you hustling, and give you that second wind.

- **Enhances Focus:** Music can help tune out distractions—whether it's a stray ball from the next court or the occasional dog barking in the distance. With your favorite beats in the background, you're locked in, focusing on the next shot and keeping your rhythm.

- **Builds Community:** Let's not forget how music sets the tone for fun! Pickleball is all about community and connection, and what better way to create that vibe than with a shared playlist? It's an instant icebreaker, a way to pump up the group, and get everyone enjoying the game together.

11.2 The Art of Setting Up the Perfect Pickleball Playlist

Now, we all know a good playlist is essential, but there's also some etiquette involved when introducing music to your pickleball game. You want to enhance the experience, not overwhelm it. Here's how to do it like a pro:

- **Bring a Bluetooth Speaker:** A portable Bluetooth speaker is your best friend here. It's small, easy to connect, and lets you control the music from the sidelines. Make sure to position it in a central spot so everyone can enjoy the tunes without it being too intrusive.

- **Keep the Volume Just Right:** While it's tempting to crank up your favorite pump-up jams, it's important to remember that pickleball is a social sport. Keep the volume at a level where it energizes the game, but doesn't drown out conversation or distract players on neighboring courts. You want the music to set the tone, not take over the show!

- **Choose Your Playlist Wisely:** Not everyone loves the same genre of music. One person's heavy metal might be another's migraine. Stick to upbeat, universally appealing tracks—think top hits, classic rock, dance tunes (yes, some players dance in between serves!) or funky throwbacks. Bonus points if you throw in a couple of pickleball-themed songs!

11.3 Why Music and Pickleball Are the Perfect Match

Pickleball is a sport that thrives on rhythm and fun—two things that music delivers in spades. When you've got a good beat driving you forward, you'll find yourself playing with more confidence, more swagger, and most importantly, more enjoyment. Music helps create a lighthearted atmosphere, making the game feel like less of a competition and more of a dance party with paddles.

Plus, let's not forget the social aspect. Music has a way of bringing people together. Between serves, there's nothing like nodding along to a great song or throwing in a quick shuffle dance move before getting back into the action. It lightens the mood, keeps everyone smiling, and can even become part of your pickleball crew's signature style.

So, the next time you're packing up your gear for the court, don't forget your secret weapon: the perfect playlist. Whether you're jamming out to classics or discovering new favorites, music has the power to take your pickleball experience to the next level. Just remember to keep it fun, keep it light, and keep it in tune with the game!

11.4 Special Bonus: My Curated Pickleball Playlist of Over 2000 Songs!

As an avid music lover, I've spent countless hours over weeks and months crafting a universally loved pickleball playlist. The result? Over 2000 songs, spanning 24 hours, guaranteeing a wide variety of tunes for your pickleball matches. Just go to this link to **listen to the playlist,** or you can find my profile, **Pickleball Enthusiast,** on Spotify. https://open.spotify.com/playlist/7gSupq VmyXeGhrhIqTQkDz?si=1695f8426b2942d2

Music is my passion, almost as much as pickleball, and I've poured my heart into creating this playlist to bring you joy, fun, and the ultimate soundtrack for the game. Enjoy!

CHAPTER 11

The Future of Pickleball

12.1 Trends in Equipment and Play

Pushing Boundaries with Tech

Pickleball, while rooted in tradition, is not immune to the relentless march of technology. Manufacturers are continuously innovating, merging science with sport to enhance player performance and experience.

- **Next-Gen Paddles:** Graphene-infused cores, aerodynamic designs, and customizable grip technologies are all making their way into paddle construction. The goal? To provide players with tools that offer maximum power, control, and comfort.

- **Weather-Resilient Balls:** Durable balls engineered to maintain consistent bounce and trajectory regardless of temperature or humidity are a boon, especially for players in varying climates.

- **Smart Footwear:** Shoes designed specifically for pickleball are seeing upgrades, too, focusing on grip, cushioning, and agility enhancement.

Smart Courts

The concept of intelligent environments extends to the sporting arena. Imagine playing on courts with:

- **Embedded Sensors:** These can track ball speed, bounce consistency, and player movements.
- **Digital Scoreboards:** Automatically updating in real-time, with instant replay features.
- **Interactive Coaching Systems:** Offering real-time feedback on player performance, helping them rectify mistakes on the fly.

12.2 Inclusion in Multi-Sport Events

Pickleball's Rising Stature

The global sporting community is taking note of pickleball's widespread appeal and competitive nature.

- **The World Games:** As a conglomerate of various sports not yet in the Olympics, the World Games could soon witness pickleball's inclusion, given its growing global footprint.
- **Olympic Dream:** With the sport's increasing popularity and competitive structure, it's not far-fetched to envision pickleball players vying for Olympic gold in the future. It might just be a matter of when, not if.

12.3 Global Expansion of the Sport

Pickleball's Global Paddle Print

No longer limited to North America, pickleball is gaining fans and players worldwide.

- **European Enthusiasm:** Countries like Spain and Italy, with their rich racquet sports history, are opening courts dedicated to pickleball, hosting tournaments, and forming national teams.

- **Asian Affinity:** Nations like India, with its penchant for badminton and table tennis, are finding a new love in pickleball, leading to the establishment of dedicated clubs and training camps.

- **Oceania Onboard:** Australia and New Zealand, known for their sporting spirit, are introducing pickleball at grassroots levels, ensuring a bright future for the sport down under.

12.4 The Future of Pickleball Broadcasting

As the sport grows, so does the audience's appetite for professional broadcasting.

- **Live Streaming:** With platforms like YouTube and Twitch, professional and amateur tournaments alike are reaching viewers worldwide.

- **Pickleball Podcasts and Shows:** Dedicated shows, where experts discuss techniques, interview players, and debate the latest in pickleball, are becoming mainstream.

- **VR and AR Experiences:** Immersive tech could soon allow fans to experience games from a player's perspective or even train in virtualized, pro-level matches.

In the grand tapestry of sports, pickleball is weaving its unique, vibrant thread. As equipment advances, global adoption increases, and potential Olympic dreams take shape, the future of pickleball looks brighter than ever. Whether you're a casual player or a seasoned pro, there's never been a more exciting time to be part of the pickleball community.

Conclusion

And so, we've reached the match point of our pickleball journey. From its backyard beginnings to the burgeoning global phenomenon it's transforming into, this sport is so much more than just paddles and specifically designed plastic balls. Every chapter you've navigated through has set you on a path of discovery, diving deep into the techniques, the communities, the trends, and the endless possibilities that the world of pickleball offers.

What truly stands out, though, is the sport's essence: it's the camaraderie, the laughter, the shared ambition, and the mutual respect that make pickleball unique. It's the way a simple game can bridge generational gaps, foster new friendships, and even open doors to business opportunities. In essence, it's a microcosm of life, played out on a court.

Perhaps you're just starting, taking those tentative first swings. Maybe you've already felt the adrenaline of a close match or the satisfaction of a well-executed dink. Or possibly, you dream of standing on the podium, medal around your neck, basking in the applause. Regardless of your ambitions, always keep in mind the heart of pickleball: it's about people as much as it is about points.

So, lace up those shoes, select that perfect paddle, and rally your loved ones or newfound friends. Whether you're diving in for the sheer joy, championing a charitable cause, or training your sights on competitive glory, pickleball beckons. Dive into this game of skill, strategy, and spirit. Ready to serve? Game on!

Sample Training Drills

Ready to refine your skills and dominate the court? These tested and proven drills are the secret weapons of top players to transform your game:

1. **The Side-to-Side Drill:** This helps improve footwork and agility. Stand at the center of your court and have a partner hit balls alternately to your left and right, requiring you to move laterally to hit them back.

2. **The Third Shot Drop Drill:** A partner hits groundstrokes to you while you practice dropping the ball softly over the net into the non-volley zone. The goal is to get the ball to bounce twice before your partner can hit it.

3. **The Dink Drill:** Both you and your partner stand at opposite ends of the kitchen. Engage in a dink rally, aiming to maintain a streak of controlled, successful dinks.

4. **The Serve-and-Return Drill:** One player serves, and the other returns. After the

return, the point is played out. Rotate serving every five points.

5. **The Volley-to-Volley Drill:** Stand about halfway to the net, and have your partner stand the same distance on the other side. Engage in a volley rally without letting the ball bounce.

6. **Overhead Smash Drill:** One player lobs the ball, trying to place it deep into the opposite court, while the other player practices smashing it back with force.

7. **Service Accuracy Drill:** Set up targets (like cones or hoops) in different parts of the service box. Practice serving to hit these targets, focusing on both depth and width.

8. **Kitchen Control Drill:** Engage in a rally where the only goal is to keep the ball within the kitchen. Any ball that bounces outside or is volleyed loses the point.

9. **Return Depth Drill:** The server serves, and the returner tries to return the ball deep into the server's court, ideally within 3 feet of the baseline.

10. **Forced Error Drill:** One player drives the ball hard and low, attempting to force their opponent into a mistake, while the other player focuses on returning the ball accurately despite the force.

Glossary of Terms

- **Ace:** A serve that is neither touched nor returned by the opposing player, resulting in a point for the server.
- **Backspin:** Spin applied to the ball where the top moves toward the player, often causing the ball to bounce backward or stop abruptly upon hitting the ground.
- **Dink:** A dink is a soft, underhand, controlled shot hit from near the kitchen line, intended to land in the opponent's kitchen (non-volley zone). It keeps the ball low and forces opponents to hit upward, slowing down the pace of play.
- **Drive:** A low, hard, horizontal shot that travels quickly over the net.
- **Fault:** A serve or shot that fails to land within the opponent's designated court area.
- **Kitchen:** The colloquial term for the non-volley zone, which is a 7-foot area adjacent to the net on each side.

- **Lob:** A lob is a high, arcing shot that sends the ball deep into the opponent's court, typically over their heads. It's used to push opponents back or take advantage of their positioning near the net.

- **Paddle:** The solid racket used in pickleball, generally made from composite or wooden materials.

- **Poach:** When a player crosses over into their partner's area to play a ball during a doubles match.

- **Pickleball:** The specifically designed, perforated, plastic ball used in pickleball. While pickleballs are slightly similar to wiffle balls in that both are perforated plastic balls, they are not the same. Pickleballs are specifically designed for the sport of pickleball, with different sizes, weights, and hole patterns than wiffle balls, which are typically used for backyard baseball or other casual games.

- **Rally:** A sequence of back-and-forth shots between players.

- **Redrop:** A defensive shot that is softly played back into the opponent's kitchen after they have attacked with a drive or a smash.

- **Serve:** The underhand stroke used to put the ball into play at the beginning of each new point.
- **Smash:** A hard, overhead shot, often hit with a downward trajectory.
- **Stacking:** A strategy used in doubles where players position themselves on one side of the court regardless of which player is serving.
- **Third Shot Drop:** A third shot drop in pickleball is a soft shot hit on the third shot of a rally, designed to land in the opponent's kitchen (non-volley zone). The goal is to slow the game down, forcing your opponents to hit upwards, allowing you and your partner to move up to the net for better positioning. It's typically used after the serve and return to neutralize your opponent's advantage. Focus on a gentle, controlled swing and aim for the ball to just clear the net and land softly in the kitchen.
- **Unforced Error:** A mistake or missed shot that is not due to the opponent's skill or shot but rather a player's own error.

- **Volley:** Hitting the ball before it bounces on the ground while standing outside the kitchen. You cannot ever volley a ball in the kitchen! It must always bounce first.

List of Resources and References

Websites

USA Pickleball Association: The governing body for pickleball in the United States, providing official rules, rankings, and tournament organization.

Pickleball Central: A comprehensive site for all things pickleball, including equipment and educational material.

Books

"The Art of Pickleball" by Gale H. Leach: A detailed guide covering the techniques, strategies, and rules of pickleball.

"Pickleball Fundamentals" by Mary Littlewood: A book focusing on the basic fundamentals of pickleball, suitable for beginners and intermediate players.

Scientific Articles

Journal of Sports Science and Medicine: "Pickleball: An Analysis of Movement and Physiological Demands": Academic paper exploring the physical demands and movement patterns in pickleball.

Medicine & Science in Sports & Exercise: "Pickleball by Older Adults: An Analysis of Anticipatory Behavior and Physical Engagement": Research paper focusing on how older adults engage with pickleball.

Made in United States
Troutdale, OR
04/11/2025

30511697R00076